MORBID
POETRY

A Nostalgic Romp

MORBID
POETRY

A Nostalgic Romp

MORBID POETRY

A Nostalgic Romp

Christin Siems Ross

WALNUT STREET
—PUBLISHING—

Design by Amelia Peterson

ISBN 979-8-9909790-4-8

Walnut Street Publishing
1645 S Holtzclaw Ave
Chattanooga, TN 37404

For my family:

the one I was born into

the one I joined

&

the one that found me

1 John 3:1

Anybody who has survived his childhood has enough information about life to last him the rest of his days. If you can't make something out of a little experience, you probably won't be able to make it out of a lot.

Flannery O'Connor

MORBID POETRY

A Nostalgic Romp

POOR UNLOVED CHILDREN

Sometimes
We would drop
Breadcrumbs
Around the house
And pretend we were
Poor unloved children
Lost in the woods
And sometimes
We did this
Naked
I think
I can't remember
And then
Mom would yell at us
"HEY
Pick up those
BREADCRUMBS!
And do the
DISHES!
And put some
CLOTHES ON!"
And we did
All the while
Plotting
To push her
Into the fire

This is what I
Tell people
When they ask me about
My childhood

SUPERSTITION

Today
I made my bed
So that
I wouldn't die

SUPERSTITION PART II

Today
I did not make my bed
A suicide attempt?
Perhaps

GOD'S LOVE

We didn't get
Any presents
Just a big box labeled
"For the Whole Wide World"
And when we'd
Open it
And see that it was
Empty
Our parents would
Gasp
And tell us
It was FILLED
To the BRIM
With
GOD'S LOVE
And we'd cry
And they'd
Go get
The real presents

OVERHEARD AT A SUPPORT GROUP FOR 90'S KIDS WHOSE DADS SUDDENLY AND WITHOUT WARNING SHAVED OFF THEIR MUSTACHES

One day the bus dropped us off at home and there was
A man in the yard raking leaves and my sister asked him
Who are you? / That happened to me! My parents
Dropped us off all summer at our grandparents' house
In Michigan and one day a man came to pick us up and
Take us home but we refused to go with him / My dad
Accidentally shaved one side of his / His what / You must
Say it / His mustache so he had to commit / I had never seen
My dad's upper lip / Unrecognizable / We hated it / We
Thought we were being kidnapped / My sister asked him to
Put it back on / So traumatized / How many more of us are
Out there? / He looked like his brother, so we called him
Uncle Steve until he grew it back.

EASTER, AGE 8

We found him
This morning
The day Christ was risen
And he was slain
By my backyard cats
My cuddly
And cute
Backyard cats
Now carnivorous
Cracked-out
Backyard killers

We found him
In the green
Among the pink
And blue
And yellow eggs
"He's just sleeping"
Dad said
As he grabbed a shovel
And shoved me inside
Before shoving him
Over the fence
While I watched
From the window
My childhood belief
Lifted with a shovel
Raised to the heavens
Suspended in mid-air
Before landing with

A thud
On the other side

We found him
This morning
The day Christ was risen
And he was slain
The Easter Bunny
Baptized in blood
Mangled and chewed
By my backyard killer cats
But I don't cry
I just eat my eggs
And my candy
In communion
To him
And at church later on
We will say
He is risen!
He is risen, indeed!
When I really know
That he is lying
Dead
On the other side of the fence

ALONE. AGAIN? DANGIT

It looks like
I'll be by myself
Forever
Because
As my mother likes to say
I'm a "handful"
And I
"Have a demon living inside me"

MAYBE I SHOULD BE A NUN

And that's the poem
Right there

MIDDLE SCHOOL NEAR DEATH EXPERIENCES

In 6th grade
I got clear braces
Which turns out
Are not clear
At all
Just make your teeth
Look bigger
And yellow

In 7th grade
I ate a hotdog too fast
Because I didn't want to
Ruin Heather's dad's
Nice new car
So
While they waited for me
To get in
I experienced
Death by hotdog
And thought
I would rather die
Than let Heather
See me choke

In 8th grade
One time
I forgot to wear
Deodorant

MY BROTHER SAYS THE F-WORD

He's fourteen
And my parents are
Acting like it's
A PHASE

It's not

They pretend to ignore him
As he walks through the house
With his new phrase of choice
"F-This"
"F-This"
"F-This"
Just loud enough so he knows
They heard him

It's not a phase

He's just developed a more articulate
Way of communicating
His contempt
For being born into our family
I mean
At least he doesn't
Hit us
Anymore

I ask my parents why
They don't do anything
Send him to his room
Ground him

Or smash up his computer
And they mumble something
About kids blah blah
Should have worn a condom
Blah blah blah

If I said the F-Word
When I was fourteen
I would have been
Spanked
Grounded
Disinherited
And cut off
From all the things
That gave me any glimmer
Of joy in my life
Like
Trips to the mall
And
My toes

What kind of double standard
Is going on here?

It's not a phase

He'll say it
Tomorrow
And the next day
And by this weekend
He'll do
Drugs
He'll try

ALL OF THEM
Because the F-Word
Is the gateway
To self-destructive behavior
Right?

Or ...
Is it
The bridge
To freedom?

I don't know
Because
When I was fourteen
I never actually
Said it
I just
Thought it
Like
All the time

MY BROTHER'S ORIGIN STORY

It makes sense
That while he was happily
Growing in our mother's
Womb
My sister and I would catch
Lice

And Mom
Didn't know how to handle
Bugs in our hair
Poison shampoos
And our little cries
Of why God why
So her body
Collapsed
And she went into
Labor

Dad was watching TV
With Mom bent
Over the couch
Begging to go
Get that sweet
Epidural relief
But he
Was watching a building
Implode
And this was before
You could pause it

Hold on, he said

It's going to go
Any minute
And I don't know how
Mom didn't
Kill him

The building imploded
Mom went to the hospital
But not in time
For sweet epidural relief
And my brother came
So fast
So angry
So red
So vengeful

If he could speak
He would have screamed
The F-word
But he was too mad
To even cry
With his fists so tight

And that
Was just the beginning

DOPPELGÄNGER

Whenever anyone tells me
I look like Maggie Gyllenhaal
I remember my first time
Hearing that

It was the first week
Of my first year at college
And a cute boy in theatre class
Told me I looked just like her

"Who is Maggie Gyllenhaal?"
I asked—and so
He invited me back to his dorm
To watch a movie

If you think you know where this is going
You don't

Did we watch Donnie Darko?
No
Did we watch Batman?
No—it wasn't out yet

We watched Secretary
And I have never been more mortified
To see my likeness do so many things
I had never seen before

Needless to say
Clay and I didn't date

SOMETIMES IT'S FUN TO BE THE FAMILY ANOMALY

When I go home
In November
And we have a family meal
I will tell my engineer parents
And my engineer sister
And my future engineer brothers
That I want to die

I will say this
Then pause dramatically
Before adding
"In the Shakespearean sense"

They will tell me to lighten up
And stop being so
Morbid all the time
And while I'm at it
Could I get a real job
Change my political views
And pass the salt?

I will laugh
(At them
Not with them
They won't be
Laughing)
Because they don't get it
They just
Don't get it

17

ROSS

Do you remember
When you ate a bug
For me?
It was some kinda
Cockroach
Or cricket
I don't know
It was ugly
And we were with
All our friends
Outside that coffee
Place we loved
Because it wasn't
Starbucks
We were sipping lattes
And talking about
Stupid teenage stuff
Like "dreams"
And "romance"
And the teachers
We hated
Do you
Remember this?

I said
"Hey Ross
Eat that bug
It will be
Funny"
And you
Picked up

The ugly bug
And you
Actually
ATE IT
And it
WAS
Funny
Kinda
But mostly
I was fifteen
And a horrible
Person
Remember that?

WHY did I ask you
To EAT
A BUG?

You were the first
One ever to say
To me
"I adore you"
I think I said
"Thanks"
And then
I made you eat
A bug

WHY?

You know
I still listen
To your music

And I can hear
In the early CDs
Subliminal messages
Of how much
You loved me
And then
In the later ones ...
Of how much
You hated my guts

I don't blame you
I made you eat
A bug

And I want you to know
I'm not proud
Of this fact
And maybe you never
Think about it
Anymore
But I
Do
And it makes me
Smile
Sometimes
That someone would
Eat a bug
To prove that they
Loved me
Probably
Nobody else
Will
And

Well
I want you to know
I'm sorry

THE SKI BABY

I'm 23
Learning to ski
Crying
And begging
Mom and Dad
To pick me up

But he—

He plows down
The mountain
Without sticks
Or fear
Or any parental supervision
In sight

He may be
Two feet tall
And cute
In his little jumper suit
But he almost
Killed me
On his reckless path
Of toddler doom

Down and down
Leaving no trail
No tracks
No apologies

Just the smell
Of a diaper
Unchanged

A LESSON FOR THE ADVENTUROUS

When you jump headfirst
Into a deep, dark pit
You should probably know
How deep
How dark
And if there is anything
Living inside
Because there might be
Lions
And they might
Eat you up
You just
Never know
These things
Happen
All the time

FRITZY'S FIRST FLIGHT

Fritzy the Goose was too scared to fly
The chill in the air was his alibi
His poor mom wanted him out of the nest
But Fritzy would cry and sharply protest:

"It's freezing, Ma! It's like fifty below!
The wind could kill me! Look at the snow!
Do you really expect me to fly out there?
Do you love me, Ma? Do you even care?

I could leave the nest, I could say adieu
But I'll catch a cold, or worse ... bird flu!
It will be all your fault, and as you watch me die
You'll think, why oh why, did I make him fly?"

So Fritzy never learned to fly with the rest
His gullible mom let him stay in the nest
He grew lazy and fat, eating grain all day
That the lazy and fat kids threw into the bay.

Until one day his mom said, "Enough is enough!"
She decided right then that love must be TOUGH.

"Fritzy, you goose, it's time to go!
I don't care if you fly through wind or through snow!
No more, no more, I won't let you stay
You're getting lazy and fat, eating grain all day."

Fritzy cried at her words (and you would too)
But he didn't whine or mention bird flu
He simply waddled out of the nest

And decided, okay, he'd fly with the rest.

But how? ... How does a goose learn to fly?
How does a fat goose lift wings to the sky?
He looked around, asking, "God, give me a sign"
And God sent Flight Fifteen Forty-nine.

"What a bird!" said Fritzy, "Look at it go!
I could follow that bird through wind or through snow!
It's a pretty big bird, so I won't have to worry
If I get lost in the clouds or a bit of snow flurry."

With his eye on the "bird," Fritzy rose from the ground
"Goodbye, Ma!" he said, "I'll see ya around!"

His mom was too proud to say it was a plane
Or that the forecast that day was freezing rain
From her now empty nest she said goodbye
Wishing Fritzy the best, with a tear in her eye.

And Fritzy flew! For about two seconds he flew ...
Until Flight Fifteen Forty-nine came cutting through
Scooping up Fritzy on its way to Charlotte
Killing the engine and staining it scarlet.

The plane had to have an emergency landing
The pilot was a hero, they called him outstanding
And everyone survived to tell of that day
Everyone but Fritzy, who wasn't okay ...

His body was smashed up, his poor neck was sliced
He suffered as much (if not more) than Christ
But do we talk of Fritzy? Do we mention his name?
No, why should we? We feel bad for the plane.

Oh poor Fritzy, most unfortunate goose!
Remember his alibi—the "chilly air" excuse?
He may have succeeded to fly with the rest
But I bet his mom wished he had stayed in the nest.

MY COMPUTER IS GIVING ME CANCER

My computer
Is giving me cancer
I know this is true
Because after sitting in front of it
For hours and hours
I get nauseous
And my head hurts
My throat goes dry
And I can't remember my name

Maybe now that I'm dying
Nobody will mind
That I have writer's block
And haven't written anything
I mean
How could I?
When all this time
My computer
Was giving me
Cancer

I hope
Someone will bring me flowers
And balloons
The metallic kind that say
"Get Well Soon"
Or
"You Are So Special"
I will sit in my hospital bed
And watch them slowly
Deflate

And think how once
I was a writer
And would still be
Writing
Great things, probably
A play
A poem
Maybe a sentence
Even a word
If only my computer
Stupid computer
Hadn't given me
Cancer

And if I recover
(I won't
It's Bad Cancer)
But if I do
I will probably
Switch careers
And be a pilot
Because pilots don't have to do
Any writing
Do they?

NO, GRANT LOKEY, I WILL NOT MARRY YOU

Because you made fun
Of my arm hair
That's why

I hardly have ANY
Arm hair
And yet
You still found a way
To make me feel
Bad about it

What?
You don't remember
Emitting Chewbacca sounds
Every time I sat next to you
In class?

What?
You don't remember
Petting me on the arms
Like you would pet your
Shaggy-haired cat?

What?
You don't remember
Stroking those arms and saying

"Oh
That is SO SWEET
What you're doing
For Locks of Love"

You don't remember that?

Well I'm sorry
That's just
That's why
I just
I just can't

I can't
Marry you

I mean
Aren't you
Allergic?

NOT AUTOBIOGRAPHICAL

"Bustache is a bus with a mustache
And IBS"
Says the first line
Of my first children's book

And the fact that I'm writing this
Has nothing whatsoever
To do with my Sriracha habit
And the acid
Eating holes in my stomach lining

It has nothing
Whatsoever
To do with my anxiety
Not unreasonable, very intestinal
Anxiety
That every time I go for a walk
A squirrel will jump from a tree
But instead of landing in another tree
The squirrel will land on me

It has nothing
Nothing
Nothing whatsoever
To do with the kamikaze antibiotics they forced me to take
Because some nutjob doctor
Diagnosed me with a penicillin allergy
When I was a kid

"You're not allergic to penicillin"
Says this doctor today

"Have you tried meditation?"
Says this doctor today
"Maybe you shouldn't eat every meal with Sriracha"
Says this doctor today

All my good gut flora is DEAD
And Bustache has IBS
But Bustache is not about ME
I don't have a mustache

SEMI-ATTRACTIVE GUY

O Semi-Attractive Guy
You semi-caught my eye
Before I bumped you with my car
While you were strutting to the bar

But I feel I have to mention
You were only semi-paying attention
And if you want to play this game
Your semi-idiocy is to blame

You may be on a semi-crusade
To get semi-drunk and semi-laid
But that doesn't mean you can semi-glare
Or look at my Civic with that semi-hate stare

(Did you think I'd semi-care?
No, Semi-Attractive Guy
No
I don't)

Do you want to know what I foresee in your life?
Ten years from now your semi-faithful wife
Who bore you three semi-lovable babies
All plagued with semi-contagious scabies

She's going to wake up one day and she'll see
That semi-hate glare you once gave to me
And she's going to say to herself: "Oh My Gawd
Is this all this guy is ... a semi-warm bod?"

And she will DIVORCE YOU

And leave you with
The SCABIES
I mean
Babies

Because guess what, Semi-Attractive Guy?

Listen close, this is no semi-lie ...
Your semi-faithful wife
DOESN'T WANT your semi-LIFE

And neither do I
Semi-Attractive Guy
Neither
Do
I

(But honestly I wasn't trying
To kill you
Please don't sue me)

WHEN YOU'RE AT THE BEACH THIS MEMORIAL HOLIDAY WEEKEND I HOPE YOU THINK OF ME AND GET EATEN BY A SHARK

This is the title of my next
Children's book
Designed to help
Little children
Get over the fact
That they have
No Friends

It will have pictures
Of happy groups of friends
Being slowly stalked
And eaten
By water-dwelling creatures
And will feature a foreword
By my 2nd-grade teacher Mr. Thurman
Who told me I had
A Beautiful Voice
And told my mother I had
No Friends

ADVICE FOR MORBID AMATEURS

So
You have a knack
For writing
And you aspire towards
The morbid
I like that
But before you write
Your next bestselling
Work of gloom
Here are some things
To think about:

ONE.
Absolutely anything
Can be morbid poetry
If it includes a metaphor
And a bitter outlook
On life
For example
The way my toast burnt
Slightly around the edges
Could relay
How my soul feels
This morning
And would make an
EXCELLENT
Morbid poem

TWO.
If you're writing
About someone you hate

Don't use their NAME
Unless getting punched
Would inspire more creative
Expression
And remember this:
If you're not specific
Everyone will think
You are writing about
Them
Which is more fun
Anyway

THREE.
Use puns
Sparingly
Puns are not
Funny

FOUR.
Floss every night
Before you go to bed
You'll live longer
And the world needs
Morbid poets
Who actually make it
Past their twenties

Finally
FIVE.
Always write the truth
Nobody cares for a poem
About a painful breakup
You had with the neighbor

You always loved
If there was no breakup
No neighbor
And no pain
So if you must write that poem
Go date your neighbor
And then breakup
And hope to God
It's painful
If not
Shoot yourself in the foot
And you can probably still write
A decent morbid poem

And that's about all
For now

So GO
Morbid Amateurs!
Put pain to paper
Write away
The cruelties of this world
And the misery of being
Young
Healthy
And tragically good-looking
Oh wait
That's me
But you know
What I mean

JOE SAYS I'VE LOST MY MORBID

"That's sweet"
He said
When he finished
Reading

"But it's not
Well
It's not
Morbid"

Uh.

"Aren't you
Supposed to be
Like
A Morbid Poet?"

Yes
I think so
I thought so
I don't know anymore

"No
I like it
It's just
Well
Never mind"

Joe thinks
This conversation
Is over

But tonight
When I creep
Into his room
With the blade
Of the sharpest kitchen knife
Pointed
Towards his neck
Maybe
He'll
Take it
Back

THE YOGA LISP LADY

On the first day
The Yoga Lisp Lady
Peered through her triple-thick
Mommy glasses
And warned me
"Thith clath ith
NOT
For beginnerth"
I was scared
Until I saw her
Hidden in the back
Relaxing in Child's Pose
While the rest of us
Saluted the Sun
And broke our bodies
Into unnatural bends
Like Gumby

And the day
We put our feet behind
Our heads
Where was she?
The Yoga Lisp Lady
Had mysteriously
Disappeared
And we never saw
Her again
Because I guess
Thith clath
Wath NOT
For beginnerth

And she had warned me ...
Oh well
Namathe

MRS. COLLINS KILLED HER MAN

Mrs. Collins killed her man
Ran him down with the family van
Before she done it, she told him "Boy,
I love you much, you bring me joy—

But I was made to wander free
And all I've seen is Tennessee
The things you promised and said we'd do
Like go to Egypt and Asia too—

Well, we're still here, we haven't gone
And I dream of pyr'mids all day long
So I'm taking the van, you can have the kid
Make him floss every night like I always did."

She got in the van, and turned on the gas
But Mr. Collins wouldn't let her pass
He told her, "Babe, I'm a simple man
But HOW can I LIVE without my van?"

She said, "Ugh, you boys from Tennessee
Get out of my way, I'll count to three ..."

ONE, but he stood there staring at her
TWO, she said, "Move or I'll kill you, sir"
THREE, he stayed and she revved up the van
And then Mrs. Collins ran over her man.

So if you dream also of pyr'mids
Go before you ever have kids
Or marry a man from Tennessee
Because Lord knows those men will be—

Happy to keep you right at home
And never let you wander or roam
Till one day you'll have to take the van
And for pyr'mids sake, run over your man.

ODE TO THE SAD, ABANDONED WEDDING BOUQUET

O Sad, Abandoned Wedding Bouquet
Who left you here
In this bathroom
To rot and decay
All by yourself?
You were not grown
Designed
And arranged
So nicely
To meet your end
Like this

O Sad, Abandoned Wedding Bouquet
Even in this classy bathroom
With pictures of Texas
On the wall
You are the saddest thing
I've ever seen
And I want nothing more
Than to take you home
And press you between two heavy books
So that your life
And your misery
Can be forever
Enshrined

O Sad, Abandoned Wedding Bouquet
Who left you here?
I really want to know ...

Who did this crime
Against love
And beauty?
Surely not
The bride
She already tossed you
To her miserably single friends
And took off in her limo
To happily married bliss
If not she,
Then who?

O Sad, Abandoned Wedding Bouquet
I cannot pretend
Anymore
It was I
It was me
I'm sorry
I left you here
In this bathroom
With pictures of Texas
On the wall
I had to do it
Because
I do not love you

O Sad, Abandoned Wedding Bouquet
I never had feelings for you at all
I did not even mean to catch you
I was drunk
And I just wanted to win
I didn't know you'd come with
So many strings attached

O Sad, Abandoned Wedding Bouquet
Please understand
That when Cousin Lisa threw you
To her miserably single friends
I didn't know what I was going for
Except that I
Didn't want anyone else to have it
I'm an evil person
I know
But you'd be upset too
If your little Cousin Josh
Caught the garter
And then refused to dance
With you

O Sad, Abandoned Wedding Bouquet
This is why that tradition should DIE
It promotes incest
And it inappropriately highlights
All the miserably single friends
I'm going to become an advocate
Right now
For the restriction of hurtful
Wedding traditions
And I'm going to start with you
Sad, Abandoned Wedding Bouquet
I'm going to start with you

THE GOLDEN RULE IS CRAP

How can I love
My Neighbor
When I don't
Even love
Myself?

And besides
He's a
Douchebag

COVER LETTER TEMPLATE FOR SINGLE, WHITE 25-YEAR-OLD FEMALES APPLYING TO MFA PLAYWRITING PROGRAMS IN THE NORTHEAST

Dear [Prestigious, Overpriced Graduate Program],

If I don't go to grad school
RIGHT NOW
I will start having
Babies.

I will marry [my loser
Ex-boyfriend/
My decade-long
Stalker/
The first guy
Who buys me
A drink],
OR
I'll just
Go Get Pregnant
It's easier than
The GRE
And the GRE is pretty
Easy
So I've heard
I take it
Next week.

I have specifically chosen this
[Prestigious, Overpriced Graduate Program]
Because I

[Have nothing better to do/
Want to go far, far
Far away
From my loser
Ex-boyfriend/
Wish to be in artist debt
For the rest of my artist
Life because I
Truly believe in the artistic power
Of depression
And starvation]
And I can't think of anyplace
Better to sow
My seeds
Of creativity
Before the seeds
To make babies
Are sown in me.

TMI?

Just let me into
Your program.

Although I won't raise
Your diversity quotient
As a Southern, Bible-Belted
Girl Who Had Braces Once,
I promise to write
Really dark, depressive
Plays that reflect that there
Truly is
NO GOD

In [Providence/
New Haven/
Boston]
And I think
You will be proud
Of me.

So
Thank you
[Prestigious, Overpriced Graduate Program]
For considering this application.

You will find attached:
My resume
Three letters of recommendation
And a used pregnancy test
That I found in a gas station
Off I-66
Please think of it
As a portent
Of [babies/
Babies/
Babies]
To come
If I don't get into
Grad school
RIGHT NOW.

I hope to hear
From you [soon/
Really soon/

Please don't
Delay/
OH MY GOD
Do Not Forsake Me]

Sincerely,

[Your name]

ON CAPITOL HILL

Here on Capitol Hill
I have learned the best
And worst
Ways to kill a conversation

If you want a conversation
To die
Try mentioning
The demons
That sometimes come
Into your room at night
And how
They shake your bed
And sit on your feet
Guaranteed
This kills conversation
Instantly

If you want a conversation
To live
However
Casually mention the rat
That swam up the pipes
Into your toilet
And how you found it
Alone
And killed it
Alive

It's amazing
People don't really want to
Hear about your demons
But they sure wanna know
How you killed
That rat

THREE REASONS WHY MORBID POETS WOULD NEVER SURVIVE LA

1. SUNSHINE
Is not the ideal climate
For a Morbid Poet

It's not that we are vampires
Really far from it
Morbid Poets enjoy a nice tan
Even a good burn
Every now
And then
Especially if the burn
Induces pain
And regret

BUT
There will be days
When you feel like stabbing
Sharp pencils
Into your heart
And honestly
HOW can you fully
Explore those feelings
With a constant stream of
Happy Vitamin D
Pouring into your bloodstream?

2. GRANT LOKEY
Currently lives there
And is probably
Still single

This is dangerous
(Refer to "No, Grant Lokey, I Will Not Marry You"
For a thorough explanation)

3. FAME
Morbid Poets
Are afraid of greatness

Unless they won a role
As a demon-possessed person
In a low-budget horror film
A Morbid Poet
Would prefer to stay out
Of the limelight
For fear that
Fame
Would overshadow
DEEP FEELING
And all morbidity
Might be lost

So
IN CONCLUSION

Morbid Poets
Must stick to the cold
Lonely
Godless
Cities of the Northeast
For survival
And sustenance
And only visit LA
For short trips
In the height
Of
Rainy season

CUBIC ZIRCONIA

I woke from a dream
Of marrying you
Relieved to find
It's Not Real

LOVE POEM FOR A MAN MADE OF IRON

I love a man made of Iron
A man not real
And soft
And light
But a man
With a heart hidden
Beneath layers
Of cold metal
Who conducts my electricity
But cannot feel
The heat

He holds me in his arms
At night
He cuddles me
Against his chest
He
Crushes me
My face
Smashed against
His steely heart
I listen
But cannot hear
The beat

And although
I can barely breathe
I whisper to him
I Love You
I Love You
I Love You

It echoes back to me
And we stay there
Like that
Lovers entwined
Me
And a man made of Iron
Stuck
Together
Like one rusted piece
Of scrap metal

MY BEST WORK YET

Another children's book I'd write
Would be about this ghost
Who was really, really
Terribly afraid
To die

The whole plot would be
That this ghost
Just stays in a closet
All day
Everyday
For all
Eternity
So basically there is really
No Plot

Yeah
Nothing really happens
It would be just, like
An inner monologue
Of the ghost
Saying how really, really
Terribly afraid he is
To die
And how he's not going to DO ANYTHING
At all
Ever
Because—
I mean—
What if he
DIES?

I think kids will
Really love it
And connect with it
On a deep level
That adults
Won't understand
Or will only
Pretend to
And I think
It might be my
Best Work Yet

Yeah
I believe it
I trust it
I just can't
Write it
Because—
I mean—
What if it's
BAD?

MY GRIEF WRITES HAIKUS

I believe my heart
Is being shredded, slowly
By a cheese grater

MARTHA STEWART SAYS

In the front cover
Of the cupcake book
You gave me
When we were still
Talking
Martha Stewart says:
Cupcakes are the treats
That make everyone
Smile

That's a bold
And very trite
Generalization
But deep down
I really believe
In Martha Stewart
And so
In the effort to move
My Stage of Grief
From Anger to Bargaining
Or at least
Depression
I baked some cupcakes

Martha Stewart says:
ANYONE
Can make cupcakes
And I think that's why
People like her
She's encouraging
And, you know

She went to jail
Which makes me smile
Even more
Than her cupcakes
But she's
Wrong
Not EVERYONE
Can make cupcakes
And cupcakes
Can't make
EVERYONE
Smile
I tried it—
I tried it—
I tried it—
And

Martha Stewart says:
There are few things
More delightfully nostalgic
Than an old-fashioned
Cupcake
Sometimes I hate
Martha Stewart
For phrases
Like that
Delightfully
Nostalgic
I'm going to gag
On this
Cupcake
Delightfully
Nostalgic

It didn't make me
Smile
Delightfully
Nostalgic
I was happier
Before I ever
Looked at this
Book
That you gave me
When we—
When we—

Delightfully
Nostalgic
What Stage
Of Grief
Is this?

ACKNOWLEDGMENTS

Thanks to Walnut Street Publishing for curating a community of artists in Chattanooga and believing in this book.

Thanks to my parents for the creepy bedtime stories and for not forcing me to be an engineer.

Thanks to my siblings for being engineers so I didn't have to.

Thanks to my husband and our three kids for allowing me to brood and disappear for a bit.

Thanks to anyone who let me vent my anxieties, or patiently listened to my fears, and then said, "this is a poem."

Thanks to anyone named or unnamed in these poems. You know who you are (hi, Grant Lokey). Thanks for the memories and the endless poetry fodder.

Thanks to anyone who supported morbid poetry in its early days, when it was just something I posted online instead of actually getting therapy. Your encouragement kept me going. But not going to therapy, that came later.

ABOUT THE AUTHOR

Christin Siems Ross flosses every night. She studied theatre at Southern Methodist University, despite the objections of her parents. Christin is a playwright, a poet, a storyteller, and hopefully one day a children's book author, but she needs better ideas. Originally from the suburbs of Dallas, she lived in DC for twelve years before moving with her family to Chattanooga. *Morbid Poetry* is her first book.

www.ingramcontent.com/pod-product-compliance
Lightning Source LLC
Chambersburg PA
CBHW012051150626
46549CB00023B/3228

* 9 7 9 8 9 9 0 9 7 9 0 4 8 *